ALL ABOUT BOAS
and other snakes

MERVIN F. ROBERTS

Cover: Miss Gretchen Lineweber with an anaconda, *Eunectes murinus*. Photo by Jeremy Dodd.

Frontis: Miss Gretchen Lineweber with a rainbow boa, *Epicrates cenchris*. Photo by Jeremy Dodd.

ISBN 0-87666-904-6

Distributed in the U.S.A. by T.F.H. Publications, Inc., 211 West Sylvania Avenue, P.O. Box 27, Neptune City, N.J. 07753; in England by T.F.H. (Gt. Britain) Ltd., 13 Nutley Lane, Reigate, Surrey; in Canada to the book store and library trade by Clarke, Irwin & Company, Clarwin House, 791 St. Clair Avenue West, Toronto 10, Ontario; in Canada to the pet trade by Rolf C. Hagen Ltd., 3225 Sartelon Street, Montreal 382, Quebec; in Southeast Asia by Y.W. Ong, 9 Lorong 36 Geylang, Singapore 14; in Australia and the south Pacific by Pet Imports Pty. Ltd., P.O. Box 149, Brookvale 2100, N.S.W. Australia. Published by T.F.H. Publications, Inc. Ltd., The British Crown Colony of Hong Kong.

CONTENTS

The ball python, *Python regius*. Photo by Jeremy Dodd.

A rainbow boa, *Epicrates cenchris*, in a dark color pattern. Photo by Jeremy Dodd.

INTRODUCTION TO BOAS

Although taxonomists vary in their treatment, this book will use the systematic basis that places the snakes commonly referred to as boas and pythons within one family, the family Boidae, in which the "true" boas are considered to comprise the subfamily Boinae (14 genera, 52 species) and the pythons to comprise the subfamily Pythoninae (7 genera, 21 species). Most snake keepers simply call all members of the family Boidae "boas," and this book will follow that practice. The true boas are found mostly in the Americas, whereas the pythons are mostly Old World snakes. Some of the 73 species of the family Boidae will be described in more detail later on, but for starters let's consider why snakes of this family make desirable pets.

To begin with, and most important, no boa is poisonous. Furthermore, if you like snakes you will surely find that boas are attractive, some positively beautiful. Large, super large or small, there is a size to fit nearly every taste. Most boas are easy to tame and live long disease-free lives in captivity. Once you get one, it should live for many years, probably longer than it would if it were in the wild. And if that is not enough, their eating habits are easy to satisfy. For example, many pet boas do nicely on thawed fresh frozen chickens, pigeons, rats, mice, rabbits, gerbils, hamsters or guinea pigs. This is easier than, for example, keeping live toads for hognosed snakes. Also, the prospective boa owner need not be greatly concerned with the ecological impact of satisfying his snake-owning desires, because in general boas are neither rare nor endangered.

If you plan to keep snakes, start with a boa; if you already have a snake of another family, look forward to getting a boa too.

SNAKES ARE GOOD PETS AND BOAS ARE GOOD SNAKES

The snake as a pet never has had a fighting chance to puts it best foot forward. One of the first mentioned animals in the Bible, it represented evil and, unfortunately, never managed to live it down. As a matter of fact, there are many present-day snakes whose dispositions are, without a doubt, characterized as evil. So much for the unpleasant side for now.

In all tropical and temperate lands except New Zealand and Ireland there are thousands of boys, and a few girls too, who annually find many beautiful and harmless snakes. These snakes make fine pets. *They are not slimy.* Many fish and amphibians are slimy, but snakes are reptiles, and reptiles are usually scaly, and never slimy. The scales of a snake are clean, dry and either keeled (rough) or smooth.

In nature there is not much black or white, but rather mostly shades of gray. That is why it is so hard to generalize and still be 100% right. However, here are a few general statements about snakes, and a few exceptions too.

Snakes are legless. (Some boas, however, have two tiny stubs at the base of the tail.)

Snakes lay eggs. (The garter snake (a fine pet) and boas, among many others, give birth to their young alive.)

Snakes are odorless. (Again the garter snake is an exception—when wild it sometimes emits a mild skunk-like scent.)

Snakes hibernate in winter. (This is true only in temperate zones. In the tropics they are almost always active.)

Snakes spit venom. (Some do, and some venomous ones don't, and some are absolutely non-venomous. The tongue of any snake is not a sting. It is 100% harmless.)

Snakes lunge at their victims. (Some do and some don't. Snakes that lunge will be able to lunge not more than one-third of their length.)

All snakes are carnivorous. (This is 100% true.)

All snakes sleep with their eyes open. (This is 100% true—they have no eyelids.)

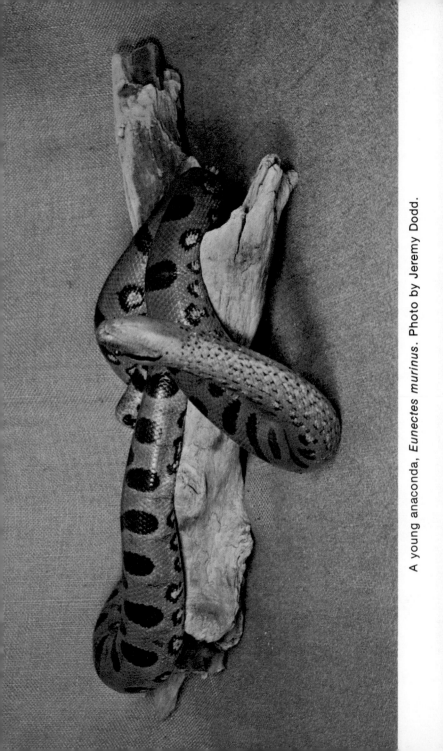

A young anaconda, *Eunectes murinus*. Photo by Jeremy Dodd.

Many of the large boas, such as this anaconda, can be easily tamed through good care and gentle handling. Photo by Jeremy Dodd.

Snakes break in half to escape enemies. (A gross misunderstanding; some will drop part of their tail tip. This story actually applies to the legless glass lizard, which looks very snake-like and has a very fragile tail more than twice as long as the body.)

There is no such thing as a hoop snake; a milk snake doesn't drink milk from the cow; snake charming doesn't depend on music; and the rattle of a rattlesnake doesn't insure anyone against anything. These facts are 100% facts.

It is a fact that when you kill a snake you have a dead snake, period. It doesn't wait until sundown or a thunderstorm to die. It simply dies when it is killed. If it crawls away it isn't dead. If it writhes after the head is severed, this is a reflex action and will soon stop.

Taxonomically, snakes are in the phylum Chordata (animals with backbones); class Reptilia (which includes cold-blooded animals that have lungs, never gills, and a three-chambered heart); order Squamata (which includes lizards and snakes and excludes all other reptiles); suborder Serpentes (which includes the snakes alone, differentiating them from the lizards because (in general) of snakes' lack of external ear openings, lack of movable eyelids, and possession of separately movable lower jaws).

CHOOSING A BOA

Selecting a boa as a pet is not too difficult, since the limitations are sharply defined. Here they are:

1.) Supply. There are no great warehouses full of many species to pick and choose from. If you are lucky you may find a dealer or a herpetological association to help you.

2.) Price. You are not likely to find any boa in a pet shop for less than $25.00. A nice fifty-pound reticulated python might sell for $200. Four dollars a pound, live weight.

3.) Size. Don't buy something you can't house. Find out how large it will become before you possess it.

4.) Habits. Start with something easy. Be sure the snake you plan to own is eating (and not regurgitating) without force feeding. Choose a species which has a good reputation for being long-lived, hardy and docile.

Boas differ from most snakes by having a vertical pupil and small, nearly granular scales on top of the head. Photo by Dr. Herbert R. Axelrod.

Let's review a short list of boas which you may encounter. Use this as a guide until your experience permits you to reach out for the more difficult species.

REGAL PYTHON. An average large specimen measures 22 feet and might weigh 225 pounds. Hard to acclimate, they are spectacular and make great pets if they can be carried over the first few months. Imported from India, they cannot be mass marketed like domestic rat snakes or water snakes.

INDIAN PYTHON. The average large specimen might be 18 feet long. It resembles the regal python. Wild specimens are mean, but most are easily tamed. This species is popular with circuses and sideshows, since it is often docile and hardy.

ANACONDA. Here an average large specimen might be 17 feet long, and a record would be anything 25 feet or over. The yellow anaconda is somewhat smaller. These snakes are less readily tamed than boa constrictors but are easily fed and live long in captivity.

Males of many species of boa have a small but distinct claw on each side of the cloaca. These are remnants of the hind legs, lost completely in most other snakes. Photo by Jeremy Dodd.

Opposite, an unidentified species of Caribbean boa, *Epicrates* sp. Photo by Jeremy Dodd.

AFRICAN ROCK PYTHON. This species is also a giant, and average large "rocks" might be 16 feet long. It is perhaps less frequently found in pet shops than the other "giants," but it makes a docile and hardy pet.

DIAMOND PYTHON. Fully grown, it might measure six to eight feet. This snake is black with a yellow spot on each scale.

BOA CONSTRICTOR. A large adult is only eleven feet long. This is one of the most beautiful of the boas. It is readily tamed and usually makes a very desirable and docile pet. The West Indian boa is a smaller, closely related species and has similar habits.

MEXICAN BOAS, *Constrictor imperator* and *C. mexicana*, are both popular among pet keepers. They are small

The reticulated python, *Python reticulatus*. Photo by G. Marcuse.

The carpet python, *Morelia* (or *Python*) *spilotes*. Photo by G. Marcuse.

The rough sand boa, *Eryx conicus*. Photo by Jeremy Dodd.

Rosy boa, *Lichanura trivirgata*. Photo by F.J. Dodd, Jr.

Eastern garter snake, *Thamnophis sirtalis sirtalis*. Photo by J.K. Langhammer.

enough to be kept in a 50-gallon aquarium. Generally speaking, they are somewhat less easy to tame than the South American forms of *Constrictor constrictor*. These two Mexican boas are usually considered to be subspecies or color variations of the wide-ranging common boa constrictor.

CUBAN BOA. Eleven feet of pure evil. Avoid this one.

RAINBOW BOA. Medium-sized boa with a good disposition and beautiful color.

BAHAMA BOA. Another medium-sized boa with good habits, it tends to be slender. Not common on the market.

TREE BOAS. Long-tailed, large-headed, beautiful and mostly nasty. A tamed tree boa is a rare and very desirable pet. The yellow species is six or seven feet, fully grown.

SAND BOAS. Blunt-tailed, small, hardy and gentle, they do well if given plenty of dry sand to burrow in. These snakes average only two feet in length.

North American boas include the RUBBER BOA, a shiny brownish species with a small head and stumpy tail, and the ROSY BOA, a larger striped species more inclined to inhabit deserts. The rubber boa is found in mountain forests north to Oregon and also in some borderline desert areas. Both are small species commonly under a foot and a half in length.

The common anaconda or water boa, *Eunectes murinus*.

Unfortunately, as you go over the list of U.S. snakes there are few boas, and these are limited in their numbers and distribution. To get yourself a boa, chances are you are going to strike a deal with another snake keeper or an importer or a pet dealer.

Here is a breakdown of the scientific names of the subfamilies and genera of the boas with the number of species and their distribution. This list is taken from Ditmars. Other authors may arrange things a little differently, but for pet keepers the arguments among taxonomists are not generally important.

FAMILY BOIDAE
Subfamily Pythoninae, the pythons

	No. of Species	Distribution
Genus *Loxocemus**	1	Mexico.
Genus *Nardoa*	1	New Ireland.
Genus *Liasis*	6	Timor, New Guinea and North Australia.
Genus *Python*	9	S.E. Asia; Africa; New Guinea and Australia.
Genus *Chondropython*	1	New Guinea.
Genus *Aspidites*	2	North Australia.
Genus *Calabaria*	1	West Africa.

Subfamily Boinae, the boas.

Genus *Epicrates*	8	Tropical America.
Genus *Boa*	6	Tropical America.
Genus *Enygrus*	4	Moluccas; Papuasia.
Genus *Trachyboa*	1	Brazil.
Genus *Ungalia*	8	Trop. So. America; West Indies.
Genus *Ungaliophis*	1	Guatemala.
Genus *Eunectes*	2	Tropical South America.
Genus *Constrictor*	8	Tropical America.
Genus *Casarea*	1	Round Island, near Mauritius.
Genus *Bolieria*	1	Round Island, near Mauritius.
Genus *Eryx*	7	No. Africa; Southern Asia.

* This is normally considered to be the only python in the New World, although it must be noted that many herpetologists no longer accept the division of the Boidae into pythons and boas but instead break the group into a number of smaller families.

Washington garter snake, *Thamnophis sirtalis pickeringii*. Photo by J.K. Langhammer.

Eastern ribbon snake, *Thamnophis sauritus*. Photo by J.K. Langhammer.

Northern water snake, *Natrix sipedon sipedon*. Photo by F.J. Dodd, Jr.

Northern brown snake, *Storeria dekayi*. Photo by J.K. Langhammer.

Genus *Lichanura* 2	Southwestern North America.
Genus *Charina* 2	Western North America.
Genus *Sanzinia* 1	Madagascar.
Genus *Morelia* = *Python*	
Genus *Corallus* = *Boa*	

COMMON AND SCIENTIFIC NAMES OF THE BETTER KNOWN BOAS AND THEIR NATURAL DISTRIBUTION

African python or African rock python	*Python sebae*	Central & South Africa
Anaconda or water boa	*Eunectes murinus*	South America
Amethystine python	*Liasis amethystinus*	Australia, New Guinea
Australian python or diamond python	*Python spilotes* or *Morelia spilotes*	Australia, New Guinea
Bahama boa	*Epicrates strictus*	Southern Bahama Islands, San Domingo
Ball python or royal python	*Python regius*	West Africa
Black-headed python	*Aspidites melano-cephalus*	Australia, New Guinea
Black-tailed python or Indian python	*Python molurus*	India, Ceylon, East Indies, China, Malay Peninsula, Java
Blood python	*Python curtus*	Asia
Boa constrictor	*Constrictor constrictor*	South America
Brown sand boa or Indian sand boa or Two-headed snake	*Eryx johni*	India

Burrowing python	*Calabaria reinhardtii*	West Africa
Carpet python	*Morelia spilotes variegata*	Australia, New Guinea
Central American boa	*Constrictor imperator*	Southern Mexico to South America
Constrictor imperator	*Constrictor imperator*	Mexico, Central America
Cook's tree boa or tree boa	*Boa endyris*	South America, West Indies
Cuban boa	*Epicrates angulifer*	Cuba, Puerto Rico
Diamond python or Australian python	*Python spilotes* or *Morelia spilotes*	Australia, New Guinea
Emerald boa or green tree boa	*Boa canina* or *Corallus canina*	South America
Egyptian sand boa or sand boa	*Eryx jaculus*	North Africa, Ionian Islands Greece, Southwest and Central Asia
Green python	*Chondropython viridis*	New Guinea
Green tree boa or emerald boa	*Corallus canina* or *Boa canina*	South America
Haitian boa	*Epicrates angulifer striatus*	Santo Domingo
Indian python or Black-tailed python	*Python molurus*	India, Ceylon, East Indies, China, Malay Peninsula, Java
Indian sand boa	*Eryx johni*	India
Madagascar tree boa	*Sanzinia madagascariensis*	Madagascar

Kirtland's water snake, *Clonophis kirtlandi* (sometimes placed in the genus *Natrix*). Photo by J.K. Langhammer.

Juvenile racer, *Coluber constrictor*. Photo by J.K. Langhammer.

Blue racer, *Coluber constrictor,* color pattern found in central U.S. Photo by J.K. Langhammer.

Striped whipsnake, *Masticophis lateralis.* Photo by F.J. Dodd, Jr.

Malayan python	*Python curtus*	Malay Peninsula
Mexican boa	*Constrictor mexicana*	Mexico, Central America
Rainbow boa	*Epicrates cenchris*	Central to South America
Reticulated python or regal python	*Python reticulatus*	S.E. Asia, East Indies, Philippines
Rosy boa	*Lichanura trivirgata*	Western North America
Rough-scaled sand boa	*Gongylophia* or *Eryx conicus*	India
Royal python	*Python regius*	West Africa
Rubber boa	*Charina bottae*	Western North America
Sand boa or Egyptian sand boa	*Eryx jaculus*	Asia, Algeria, S.E. Europe, Egypt
Tree boa or Cook's tree boa	*Boa endyris*	South America, West Indies
Two-headed snake or Indian sand boa or brown sand boa	*Eryx johni*	India
Water boa	*Eunectes murinus*	South America
West Indian boa	*Constrictor orophias*	Santo Domingo
Yellow anaconda	*Eunectes notaeus*	South America
Yellow tree boa	*Boa cookii*	Tropical S. America, Southern West Indies

There are probably six South American tree boas. Their common names and associated scientific names are confusing, and no attempt will be made here to resolve this issue.

The Indian or black-tailed python, *Python molurus*. Photo by L.E. Perkins.

NATIVE AMERICAN SNAKES

There are about 350 species (including some subspecies) of snakes in the United States, not counting Alaska and Hawaii, and 56 of them are venomous. The 56 venomous ones include:

35 rattlesnakes (*Crotalus*)
8 pigmy rattlers and massasaugas (*Sistrurus*)
5 coral snakes (*Micruroides* and *Micrurus*)
and
8 copperheads and
cottonmouth water moccasins (*Ancistrodon*)

Corn snake, *Elaphe guttata*. Photo by Dr. K. Knaack.

Western patch-nosed snake, *Salvadora hexalepis*. Photo by F.J. Dodd, Jr.

Glossy snake, *Arizona elegans*. Photo by J.K. Langhammer.

Rat snake, *Elaphe obsoleta*. Photo by F.J. Dodd, Jr.

So much for the 56 you should avoid. Let's now consider the approximately 300 non-venomous species. Included are many groups whose names help describe them.

These major groups are: rainbow, glossy, worm, scarlet, rubber boas, sand, shovel-nose, racers, black striped, sharp-tailed, ringneck, indigo, speckled racers, rat, mud, hook-nosed, earth, hognose, night, kingsnakes, cat-eyed, blind, rosy boas, swamp, whipsnakes, water, green, vine, bull snakes, slender, long-nosed, patch-nosed, black swamp, ground, short-tailed, brown, black-headed, lyre and garter snakes (*Thamnophis*). The garter snakes, genus *Thamnophis*, are found from coast to coast in nearly every one of the 48 contiguous states. There are no fewer than 41 species and subspecies of garters.

CHOOSING AND COLLECTING NATIVE SNAKES

If you obtained this booklet first and now want a native snake, the best way this author knows is to start with a young man. Any young man—about ten years old is fine—let loose in a field or woodlot on a warm sunny summer day soon will have a snake. It is as simple as that. Some pet shops handle snakes, but in many areas the above mentioned gentlemen offer such fierce competition that many pet dealers just don't bother. The boas are an exception. They are so desirable as pets and so limited in their natural range in the United States that the only way for most people to get one is to buy it in a pet shop or from another snake fancier.

The actual technique of catching a snake must start with an admonition. *If you don't know what it is—leave it strictly alone.* In the U.S. there are (taken broadly) four groups of venomous snakes. They are (1) rattlesnakes, (2) copperheads and cottonmouth water moccasins, (3) pigmy rattlers and (4) coral snakes.

A safe way to be sure is to follow this rule, which is practically fool-proof. Don't touch mottled or multi-ringed snakes. (One ring around the neck is safe.) If the design is checkerboard, diamond, squares, blotches, muddy brown, irregular, or in the last instance, several rings of various colors all the way around the body, leave it alone. *If in doubt, leave it alone.*

If a native U.S. snake has one or several long straight stripes down its entire length or is solid green or dark blue, or if it has a single light colored ring at the neck, you are undoubtedly dealing with a safe species. True, this rule eliminates several interesting pets—and virtually all native snakes but the garters, some racers, the green snakes, and the ringnecks —but until you *know* which species is which on sight, you should follow this rule.

Actually, the easiest way to learn to identify the poisonous species is to purchase any of the several small reptile identification guides available on the market. There are small books which cover the entire eastern or western United States (the Peterson *Field Guide* series), and almost every state has one or more illustrated books dealing with its snake fauna. These books will also allow you to identify any snake you find within their coverage area and often they tell you a lot about the species' diet, habits, activity period, etc.

The general shape of a snake's head is no guide to its venom or lack of it. Common non-venomous hognose snakes, water snakes, and even garter snakes can spread their heads and the rear ends of their lower jaws to appear quite formidable. On the other hand, the coral snake of our southern states hardly spreads his head at all, but his venom, drop for drop, is about as deadly as the cobra's.

Various sections of this country are populated with different species which are locally known to be good pets. The Northeast, for instance, has the green, the black, the ribbon and the garter snakes. These above are all sure to be safe. There are also plenty of hognose, water and milk snakes. The last three named might be confused with a copperhead, and since water snakes are mean anyway you might as well shy away from all three at least for a starter.

Garter snakes, incidentally, are common in many areas across the country and make fine pets wherever they are found.

In the Southeast the blacksnake, the king snake, the indigo snake and the rat snake are well known and popular. If you *know* these snakes on sight you don't need this to tell you they can be kept as pets. If there is doubt, choose one whose marks positively prove it safe.

The western states offer, among others, the western garter snake, green snakes and several ringnecked snakes.

Bullsnake, *Pituophis melanoleucus sayi*. Photo by H. Hansen, Aquarium Berlin.

Florida kingsnake, *Lampropeltis getulus floridana*. Photo by G. Marcuse.

California kingsnake, *Lampropeltis getulus californiae*. Photo by F. J. Dodd, Jr.

Catching a non-venomous snake can be done with: (1) a noose at the end of a stick (this often breaks the neck of large, active species); (2) a net and a stick (the next difficulty is getting the snake out of the net); (3) a flour sack or pillow case and a stick (not too inefficient if you can convince the snake it wants to go in); (4) a forked stick (good in an emergency, but if the fork is the wrong size the snake will either escape or will tear the delicate skin on the neck); (5) a true snakestick with a piece of angleiron or a blunt hook at the end (this is the best bet and also the safest for the snake, next to method 6); and (6) the bare hands and a light "holding help" from the sole of your shoe (the best method, although it takes practice and sometimes courage, especially with water snakes, and requires that you be absolutely certain of your identification—*never* try this with a snake suspected of being poisonous or with an unidentified tail sticking out of a hole).

A snake noose (top) and a simple snakestick made from a hoe (bottom).

The best situation from the standpoint of the snake hunter is to find a snake resting beneath a piece of sheet metal in the ruins of an old barn or scrap pile. Simply walk quietly, turning over old tins, ash cans, and pieces of corrugated roofing metal. Snakes enjoy the heat that builds up under the rusty metal on a sunny day, and if you are quick you can catch them before they get over their lethargy. Look under stones, preferably flat ones, for ringnecks and garters. Green snakes and blacksnakes are found in the open; green snakes wander in grass. Blacksnakes favor sunny woodlands.

If you find a ribbon snake or a garter snake and you are sure from the pattern that this is what it is, don't be afraid of it. It may flatten its body, coil up, rear, hiss a bit and even strike at you. Its teeth are slanted back and its jaws must be peeled off gently if you are unlucky enough to be bitten. Treat the scratch with peroxide or iodine and forget it. It isn't any more poisonous than a scratch from a rose thorn.

Garter snakes, incidentally, emit a slight musky odor when first caught. (In other words—not to be read out loud—garter snakes often stink when they are caught.) This slight odor soon passes away and is not emitted again (really!).

Most snakes in this short list of "approved native U.S. species" will quickly sense that you want to be their friend and soon become quite tame. Animal trainers and circus side show performers often make affectionate pets of their charges and even let them share their beds on cold nights. (It was about this time in the experience of the author that Mrs. Roberts decided her son would be an engineer.)

KEEPING PET SNAKES

It is vitally important to your snake that his cage permit him a chance to get into shade. Too many snakes have been cooked by keepers who unknowingly placed the cage in bright sunlight. In nature your pet could select his sun and shade. His cage must also permit him to make this choice.

Some snakes prefer a secluded place—an inverted flower pot, tipped up just a little, works nicely. In fact, without it your pet may refuse to eat voluntarily.

If the aquarium you plan to use as a cage has a side or end knocked out—so much the better—just screen it in the same way you screen the top. The additional ventilation is a worthwhile improvement. Favor plastic screening over metal.

The cage should be provided with a dish of water and a rough, heavy stone or coarse piece of bark-covered wood for your pet to rub against in order to help it to shed. Don't anticipate shedding, and don't help unless it is obvious the snake is having great difficulty. Providing a dish of water to moisten the skin is sometimes the simplest way to assist. If you shed a snake's skin before it is ready, you will surely kill it. The freshly shed snake is most colorful. His new, clean skin positively glitters and has a velvety feeling. If you plan to photograph your pet in color, the best time to do it is just after it sheds.

Zoo records show that many boas and other snakes have been kept alive for twenty years. With proper care, your pet boa should mature in two to five years and continue to grow more slowly for the remainder of its life.

Longnosed snake, *Rhinocheilus lecontei*, western United States. Photo by J. K. Langhammer.

Milk snake, *Lampropeltis triangulum*. Photo by F. J. Dodd, Jr.

Great Plains ringneck snake, *Diadophis punctatus edwardsi.* Photo by J. K. Langhammer.

Eastern hognose snake, *Heterodon platyrhinos.* Photo by J. K. Langhammer.

CAGES AND ESCAPES

Since most snakes manage to escape from most cages, this chapter will treat both subjects together.

A snake cage should be simple. This is the cardinal rule. Unless there are some special requirements, you should try to find an aquarium to serve as a cage. It is cheap and easy to clean and has only one rectangular area to be kept closed. A well made, carefully fitted, heavy screen in a rugged wooden or metal frame makes a good cover. Such a top on an aquarium is as foolproof a home for your pet as can be had. A five-gallon tank is just about large enough for a green snake. Three or four small garters or a small blacksnake will do nicely in a 20-gallon aquarium measuring 12" x 12" x 30". A 50-pound boa could be kept in a long, shallow 75-gallon aquarium.

In Ledyard, Connecticut, Mr. Robert Lineweber keeps his pet boas in wooden cages with glass front windows and screened ends and screened covers. He prefers plastic screen since his pets are less liable to rub their noses raw on plastic than on metal screen. His cage bottoms are gravel; each cage contains a water dish, and heat is provided by heating the entire snake room.

For small snakes an earth bottom with a few plants and possibly a flat stone or a piece of bark will complete the arrangements. Water should be provided, and this can be best done with a dish of water set in the earth. With a small atomizer or watering can *not oftener* than once in two weeks, just lightly sprinkle the leaves of the plants. This will more than keep the humidity at the proper level and also help the plants to grow. Of course desert snakes, and the desert plants you would keep with them, require even less water.

The cage or aquarium door or cover should be large enough to permit you to easily reach any part of the inside. It *must* be fit tightly; it is amazing how little space a snake needs to escape through. It must be heavy or well fastened. Snakes may not have extremely high intelligence, but they are first-rate escape artists. Fastening is especially important if small children or dogs, cats or other pets are anywhere in the vicinity. There is a story about Pandora and her box which is repeated time and again in every pet-keeping household. The rub about escaped snakes is that they rarely return of their own free will.

The common boa constrictor, *Constrictor constrictor*. Photo by L.E. Perkins.

Western ringneck snake, *Diadophis punctatus regalis*. Photo by J. K. Langhammer.

Spotted night snake, *Hypsiglena torquata,* western United States and Mexico. Photo by J. K. Langhammer.

Reticulate python, *Python reticulatus.* Photo by H. Hansen, Aquarium Berlin.

Blood python, *Python curtus.* Photo by J. K. Langhammer.

FEEDING

Most snakes can be trained to eat dead food. Dr. James Oliver, in his excellent *North American Amphibians and Reptiles*, suggests that it is unwise to leave a live rat or even a mouse in a cage with a snake overnight. Too often the tables are turned and the snake is the victim. If your pet is of frog-eating size consider three possibilites. First: Feed live frogs. These can be caught during at least eight months of the year in most states. In wintertime your pet may be sluggish anyhow and can subsist on possibly one meal during the four cold months; for this you can keep a frog or two alive in another aquarium. Second: Feed your pet fresh frozen frogs; thaw them just before feeding time and they will certainly be sweet and fresh. In this way you can lay up a stock of frogs during the warm weather and never lack snake food. Third: Train your pet to eat fresh raw fish; watersnakes and some garter snakes relish fish anyway. Cut pieces somewhat larger than your pet's head. You will discover that each snake prefers to be fed in his own special way. You may have to experiment; but once you succeed, stick to the system. Milk snakes eat mice. Trap mice; feed them fresh and freeze the surplus. Your pet will soon learn to accept and enjoy a dead mouse as much as he did the live wild one he previously hunted. Blacksnakes, milk snakes, gopher snakes, rat snakes and indigo snakes will all thrive on mice and small rats. Watersnakes, large garters and hognosed snakes will eat most toads, some frogs, and often the bodies of mice rubbed with a living toad to give it the proper smell. Ringnecks, green snakes, ground snakes and most other small species will do well on insects with soft bodies and on earthworms. Many can be "weaned" onto a diet of lean chopped meat mixed with earthworms and sometimes a little bit of egg yolk.

Most snakes can get around any food which is not more than twice the size of their heads. Long objects offer no problem. This should serve as a warning in case you plan to keep several sizes of snakes or a snake and several other small pets in one cage. A garter snake can easily eat a chameleon. A watersnake may quickly do away with a turtlet.

Boas range in size from babies of small species to adults of the 200 + pound giants. Their food varies as their size. A small green tree boa will do nicely on mice and road-killed small birds. When snakes get up in size and weight, the meals should come in larger sizes too.

For example:

A 45-pound African rock python might eat one 4-pound rabbit every seven days.

A young 30-pound anaconda is known to do nicely on a rat every ten days or a guinea pig every two weeks.

A 20-foot python weighing about 225 pounds has been observed eating a 40-pound pig, but this is the upper limit. Actually this specimen was generally fed two or three chickens at a meal, this only six times a year.

Most boas prefer warm-blooded prey, but this does not necessarily mean *live* birds or *live* mammals. Road-killed animals of the right size can be frozen and then thawed out the day before your pet needs a meal, or you can breed your own rats, mice, rabbits, hamsters or gerbils and if your supply gets ahead of your demand, just freeze the surplus.

Many zoos provide large bathing tanks for their boas, and these snakes are sometimes seen to remain in the water for a week or so while digesting a meal. This is not necessary; perhaps the snake found the water nearer the desired temperature than the air and went into the water only because of its warmth. Mr. Lineweber keeps most of his boas in cages with just drinking water and dry gravel. They digest their food properly and promptly, and they thrive and shed their skins on schedule, all with no bathing tanks.

The force feeding described later for small pet snakes can be applied in modified form to larger specimens. Hold the snake gently but firmly behind the head. Try a relatively small meal—possibly just a dead but still warm mouse for a 10-pound snake—and rub the head of the mouse against the lips of your snake. Press it in gently as the lips open and start it down the snake's throat, pushing with a small flat stick, like a tongue depressor or popsicle stick. Once the mouse is started down the snake's throat, it will probably continue downward through the effort of the snake. Be extremely careful not to break any teeth or cut the gums during force feeding, as this often results in bacterial and fungal infections which will kill or disfigure your pet.

Many zoo snakes are force fed all their lives in captivity, but these specimens are frequently chosen for display because

Rock python, *Python sebae*. Photo by J.K. Langhammer.

Boa constrictor, *Constrictor constrictor*. Photo by J.K. Langhammer.

Rainbow boa, *Epicrates cenchris*. Photo by G. Marcuse.

Brown sand boa, *Eryx johni*. Photo by G. Marcuse.

they are rarely seen elsewhere. For starters, pet keepers should limit themselves to simpler problems and not take on a snake unless they *know* it is eating voluntarily.

FOODS FOR SMALL SNAKES

Most of the smaller pet snakes will eat earthworms and do nicely on them. The advantages of the earthworm as a food are several and are worth understanding.

The earthworm is a complete organism. This means that all the vitamins, minerals, proteins, fats and roughage (except bone) are within its body. Raw strips of steak, for instance, represent only part of the beef and lack many important substances found mostly in, say, the digestive organs of animals.

A juvenile rainbow boa, *Epicrates cenchris*. Photo by G. Marcuse.

The earthworm is easy to manipulate and easy to feed and is available in all sizes up to five inches.

Although earthworms have been described as man's best friend (for their soil-making activities), hardly any one objects on humane grounds to their use as pet food.

Earthworms can be kept odorless and disease free, without fancy or costly equipment.

Finally, most small snakes seem to enjoy eating worms.

The trick narrows down to getting the worm from the dish into the snake's stomach. Actually it's really not very difficult. The equipment consists merely of a worm, a snake and a 6-inch broomstraw. The technique is simply to hold your pet firmly with one hand. Hold it right behind the head and support the rest of its body on a table or in your palm. With the other hand pry the jaws apart with the broomstraw and leave the straw in the snake's mouth. It should be "cross-ways" to the line of the teeth (like a bit in a horse's mouth); about three inches will extend to either side. With the mouth pried open and the straw holding it so, lay a worm on the straw. Close the mouth over the worm and the straw, slowly reducing the pressure on the straw and you increase the pressure on the jaw to close it. Withdraw the straw and now you have a snake with the middle of a worm well back in its mouth and the mouth closed. Develop your technique to do the job quickly and quietly. Do not overly upset your pet.

When the worm is placed as described, your pet snake may spit it out, but chances are it will commence to eats its dinner. If (as sometimes happens) the first trial fails, repeat it. In the event of a second failure, put it away for two days, then try again. The ribbon snake might exist on earthworms, like so many of his relatives, but his natural food is more likely to be newts, fish, frogs and other aquatic life. It is important to know something about where your pet was found in order to choose the best foods for him.

If your pet snake is less than three feet long and doesn't eat earthworms, try crickets, grasshoppers, peepfrogs and toads. Don't force-feed toads or pickerel frogs, since some have poison skins and are not palatable to all snakes. If your pet will eat crickets, your problem is solved during the summer. In winter you can breed crickets in a large tin pail—feed them on cracker meal, hay and bran. Also try mealworms. Buy a culture to get started.

Green tree boa, *Boa canina*, orange young. Photo by J.K. Langhammer.

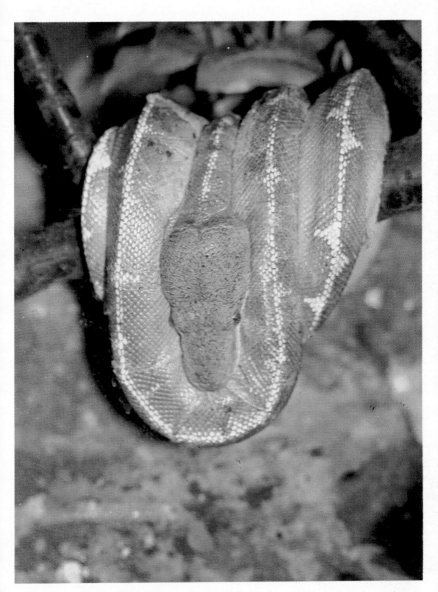

Green trea boa, *Boa canina*, adult. Photo by H. Hansen, Aquarium Berlin.

FEEDING DO'S AND DON'TS

DON'T force first, but rather try frogs, try worms, try small live fish in water.

DON'T try force feeding unless absolutely necessary.

DON'T try to force feed unless you are reasonably sure the snake is hungry.

DON'T try to feed heavy meals to your pet when he is slugfish in wintertime.

DON'T force feed "warty" toads or pickerel frogs; their skins may be repulsive or even poisonous to most snakes. The exception is the hognose. He eats most toads.

DON'T feed *two* snakes of dissimilar size *one* mouse. (The larger snake will eat the mouse and anything which may be connected to it, including the other snake.)

DO keep water before your pets at all times.

DO record the meals your pet consumes.

DO try to keep your pet fed but not stuffed.

DO release your native pet if it refuses to eat within a few days to weeks (depending on size and season) after capture. Small species seldom look "skinny" until it is too late. A dead snake gives no one satisfaction in this day of ecological awareness.

MALE AND FEMALE

All other things being equal, the male snake has a longer tail and an even taper from the body to the tip of the tail.

The female has a relatively shorter tail. A steep taper from a wider body to this shorter tail takes place at the base of her tail. Some boas have naturally blunt tails. Compare several specimens of the same species to be sure of the differences.

BREEDING

Most snakes breed once a year, in springtime, and females generally produce at least one brood as a result of that mating. In the case of egglaying snakes, the eggs are laid anytime from several weeks to years (possibly) after mating.

Eggs hatch anytime from several days to several months, depending upon species, temperature and humidity. So you see, there is no hard and fast rule. Egglaying snakes produce leathery white long ovals which are either incubated by the mother or buried in warm earth or decaying warm vegetable material. If you find snake eggs you might bury them in moist sand to a depth of one inch and keep them about 75 degrees F., but not in direct sunlight. The young are born escape artists. They start out with a horny egg-tooth which helps them to cut through and escape the leathery egg. If there is an ever-so-tiny opening in the cage, they will escape that too. Among venomous snakes the young can bite, or spit, or both, from birth and must always be considered absolutely dangerous. Soon after a hatchling is born it sheds its first skin. It will shed by itself. Don't try to help it.

Pythons lay eggs. So do most other groups. True boas (of the subfamily Boinae) are livebearers. The livebearers also include the rattlesnakes, copperheads, water moccasins (cottonmouth), common harmless garter snakes, and the common non-venomous watersnakes. Livebearing snakes are born in thin transparent sacs which burst soon after birth.

HIBERNATION

Where the air temperature remains below 32° F. for any extended periods, cold-blooded animals must hibernate in a place where it is above 32° F. or they will perish.

Most native American snakes do hibernate, and this period of dormancy or semi-dormancy depends on the degree of frost or semi-frost. The colder they think it is going to be, the lower into the earth they go. If they freeze, they die. Make no mistake about that. When they hibernate, they do not freeze. They merely become lethargic; or if even cooler—dormant. In this state they pass through cold periods buried below the frost line.

In the cage your pet will become less active as the days grow shorter. The degree of his lethargy depends on how much light and warmth (primarily warmth) he is exposed to. You can control this to suit yourself. If the winter temperature in the cage is lower than it was in your snake's natural summer habitat, you should expect it to be less active. It will shed less

Diced water snake, *Natrix tessellata*. Photo by H. Hansen, Aquarium Berlin.

Checkered water snake, *Natrix piscator*. Photo by H. Hansen, Aquarium Berlin.

frequently; it should be fed less. Overfeeding a half-hibernating snake is bad practice; it may cause stomach disorders or even death.

For boas the ideal temperature is probably about 80 or 82° F.

SHEDDING

All snakes periodically shed their skins. Actually what comes off is one thin layer of amber or nearly colorless membrane. This shedding is normal and healthy and should happen at least several times a year. Some snakes shed more frequently, especially if they are growing rapidly.

Just before a snake is about to shed, the skin takes on a lackluster milky-opalescent look. This is especially evident over the eyes.

A moist atmosphere or a bath seems to help most snakes to shed. The actual lubricant, however, is a natural "snake oil." When the skin begins to peel, it starts at the mouth and works back inside out. The skin peels off and falls free within a few hours after the operation began. Before shedding begins and the eye has the milky appearance, the snake is likely to be irritable, probably because its sight is impaired. Normally gentle snakes sometimes get nippy then, and of course had best be left alone.

FANGS AND POISONS

To withdraw the fangs of a venomous snake and thus render it harmless is parlor talk, not scientific fact. The glands which produce venom and the sacs which store it are not in or near the fangs. Removal of fangs does not destroy venom, it merely makes it somewhat harder to get the venom into the victim. Not impossible, just somewhat harder. Also to be remembered is that fangs once removed will grow back, and again the snake will be as "good as new."

There is a little ditty concerning the identification of the deadly coral snakes. It goes, "Red to yellow—kill a fellow, red to black—venom lack." This is the way the men in the southern snake country separate the sheep from the goats. The body pattern on a coral snake is yellow-red-yellow—black—yellow-red-yellow-black and so on. The red is always "next to" the yellow. Also the coral snake's head is black all the way to the eye, and the rings go all the way around the coral snake's body. Incidentally, coral snakes are found in Florida, Texas and Arizona, and as far north as western kentucky and the Carolinas.

On the other hand the absolutely non-venomous, strikingly beautiful, scarlet king snake—a near relative of the milk snakes—has many of the same colors (sometimes substituting white for yellow) but in this order: black-red-black—white (or yellow)—black-red-black—white and so on. In other words, nowhere is there a joining of red to yellow. Unfortunately, of all the king snakes, the scarlet is one of the most difficult to maintain in captivity.

SNAKE BITE

The best way to avoid snakebite poisoning is to avoid poison snakes. There are plenty of fine, fascinating, easily tamed, non-venomous snakes to keep as pets.

Very few people in the U.S. who are bitten by venomous snakes die of snake bite. Some, however, have heart attacks brought on by fear. If you know the snake that bit you was venomous, call a doctor. If swelling or nausea occurs, call a doctor. If you go into "snake country," have along a suction outfit. Read the instructions before you are bitten. Read them twice if necessary. Don't permit a bitten person to become overheated or to drink anything alcoholic. The story about whiskey as a snakebite cure is an absolute (and dangerous) myth.

If you keep large constrictors, say over six feet, you might be wise to have a large mirror in your snake room. Then if one of your pets gets draped around your neck and seems to be getting too tight, you can go to the mirror; you may be able to find an end to start unwinding.

This chapter until now has been about snakes biting men. Now is the time to turn the tables and coin the phrase of the newspaper editors—"when a man bites a dog—that's news." So let's consider snakes as they relate to people's teeth.

Oriental rat snake, *Ptyas mucosus*. Photo by H. Hansen, Aquarium Berlin.

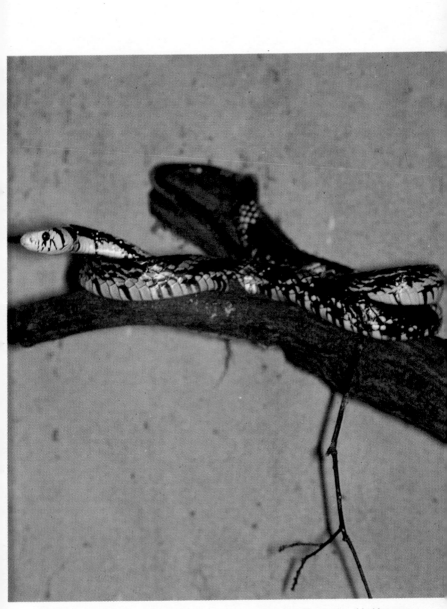

Black and yellow rat snake, *Spilotes pullatus*. Photo by H. Hansen, Aquarium Berlin.

In southern China, especially around Canton, a dish containing mostly snake-meat is esteemed by gourmets. In Hong Kong high class restaurants today, a banquet consisting primarily of snake-meat stew would be the highest priced item on the menu. Mr. Yin-Ching Au, formerly of Hong Kong, told the author that the most desirable snake meat used was that obtained from venomous snakes. The meat of the non-venomous species is considered to be of inferior quality. Here in the U.S.A. rattlesnake meat has been available for many years. It too is a high priced dish, and it too is considered a delicacy by those who know. Here also it seems the venomous snake provides the best eating.

HANDLING DO'S AND DON'TS

DON'T handle any snake that you have the slightest doubt about.

DO hold and lift your pet gently.

DO support its weight when you lift him.

DON'T wave your pet under anyone's nose or practice practical jokes with snakes.

DO be careful with harmless wild snakes; some will soil your clothing, if they can, until they become tame.

HANDLING SNAKES

Even non-poisonous snakes can be nippy. Some species, watersnakes for instance, are generally worse about this than others. Green snakes and ringnecks are often docile from the moment they are caught.

For your first experience, choose a snake you are *sure* of and grasp it firmly, *but without pinching*, right behind the head. The closer to the head you control it, the safer you are during the taming process. Lift the snake clear of the ground and promptly support its body with your free hand. Your pet will enjoy the warmth of your hand. Don't squeeze or pinch. Hold it gently but firmly. Its tongue is harmless; let your pet explore your fingers. Stand in a place where, should your pet fall, it will neither fall far nor have a chance to escape. If it has

Chondropython viridis, the green python. Photo by G. Marcuse.

Mussurana, *Clelia clelia*. Photo by G. Marcuse.

Coluber species. Photo by G. Marcuse.

Cuban racer, *Alsophis angulifer,* Cuba. Photo by H. Hansen, Aquarium Berlin.

Leopard snake, *Elaphe situla,* southern Europe and western Asia. Photo by Dr. K. Knaack.

its own cage, just work over the open top. As you gain confidence and your pet gains trust, you can continue to relax your hold without giving up control. As you and your pet become more accustomed to each other, you will begin to wonder why some people are so unreasonable about such a graceful and beautifully colored animal. This is the time to remember that there is good reason for their being "unreasonable"—many people get that way from having a "wise guy" thrust a snake under their nose. It is, to say the least, inconsiderate to humans and cruel to the snake.

MIXED SOCIETY

Many snakes are cannibalistic. Some species are 100% cannibals. They eat nothing but other snakes. The best way to keep your pets is to keep them segregated by sizes and watch them closely for any hint of unfriendly acts.

Another problem which might come up with two snakes of different sizes happens when they are eating. As already mentioned, if both commence on opposite ends of the same mouse or rat or rabbit, the larger snake might just keep going and consume his cage mate too.

KEEPING SNAKES IN TERRARIUMS

Some snake keepers want their pets in a more natural looking setting than a bare box or aquarium with a sand or gravel bottom. The answer might be a terrarium or at least some arrangement of branches or rocks or water to break the monotony of four glass or screen walls. Many small snakes may be kept with other reptiles and even some amphibians, so although this is a book about boas and other snakes, it is hard not to mention the other herptiles which may be kept with them.

A terrarium is a concentrated segment of nature. A bit of desert with cacti and sand boas and perhaps a gopher tortoise, petrified wood, dry sand, bright hot sunlight and shaded crannies. Or woodland-bog with moss, damp lichen-covered bark, turtles, and a milk snake and leafy plants which get a little filtered sunlight for a few hours a day. Or a shoreline with more or less equal areas of land and water, aquatic plants, water turtles or maybe a crocodilian or a small watersnake. Or a wholly aquatic environment, which is really an aquarium, according to the dictionary, but since this book is intended to help you house your pet dry *or* wet, it too will be discussed here. You can choose any environment you would like to bring into your home, and then pick snakes and other animals which thrive there.

What makes a desert, a woodland glen, a bog, a shoreline? Many things. Name some? Sure!

Desert: Hot dry days, cool nights often 40 degrees cooler, sometimes with dew condensing. Bright sunlight ten, twelve, or even fourteen hours a day. Sandy soil, cactus.

Bog: Moist air, uniform temperatures—maybe only ten degrees warmer in daytime. Standing water, moist earth, leafy plants.

Which do *you* want? You cannot have both in the same terrarium at one time. Luckily, all the habitats are inexpensive and fairly easy to set up. All offer wonderful animals to study. What animals?

Desert: Horned "toads," some snakes (sand boas for example), many lizards, a few tortoises, several toads, few or no frogs, no salamanders.

Woodland: Some turtles and tortoises, many snakes, many lizards (including the American chameleon or anole), some toads, many frogs, many newt efts and salamanders.

Bog: Many turtles, some snakes, few lizards, many frogs, few or no toads, many newts and salamanders.

Shoreline: Many turtles, some snakes, no lizards, but crocodilians, many frogs, few or no toads, many newts or salamanders.

Aquatic: Some softshell turtles, aquatic frogs, waterpuppies, sirens, and some swamp snakes; but no American frogs or toads, or woodland turtles or even common pond turtles like the painted or the red ear.

So now the pie is cut according to habitat. But this doesn't quite settle everything. There is still the problem of picking various kinds and sizes that get along—let's say *tolerate*—each other. For instance: Snakes have a way of eating frogs. Big frogs have a way of eating small frogs. Some

Green tree snake, *Leptophis ahaetulla.* Photo by G. Marcuse.

Green vine snake, *Oxybelis fulgidus* (top) and brown vine snake, *Oxybelis aeneus* (bottom). Photo by G. Marcuse.

Long-nosed tree snake, *Dryophis* sp. Photo by G. Marcuse.

Golden tree snake, *Chrysopelia ornata.* Photo by G. Marcuse.

turtles will eat some newts. And crocodilians eat practically anything they can swallow whole or tear apart.

Here is a listing of many terrarium pets, what environment they like, and what other animals they may be kept with.

AMERICAN CHAMELEONS (ANOLES). Best habitat: woodland. Companions: skinks, tree frogs, toads; small snakes which do not eat lizards.

CROCODILIANS (crocodiles, caymans, alligators): Best habitat: shoreline. Companions: none but same-size brothers.

FROGS FOR FOREST HABITAT: wood frog, spring peeper. Companions: other same-size frogs and toads, turtles.

FROGS FOR BOG HABITAT: spring peeper. Companions: other same-size frogs and toads, turtles.

FROGS FOR SHORELINE HABITAT: green frog, bullfrog. Companions: other same-size frogs, turtles.

LIZARDS FOR DESERT HABITAT: horned lizards, leopard lizards, swifts. Companions: gopher tortoises, sand snakes.

LIZARDS FOR FOREST HABITAT: skinks, fence lizards. Companions: other same-size lizards, turtles, same-size snakes.

NEWTS: Bog or shoreline habitat. Companions: same-size frogs.

SALAMANDERS: bog habitat. Companions: small frogs.

SNAKES FOR FOREST HABITAT: garter, green, ringneck. Companions: same-size snakes and lizards.

SNAKES FOR BOG HABITAT: milksnake, water snake. Companions: same-size snakes and lizards.

SNAKES FOR SHORELINE HABITAT: ribbon snake, watersnake. Companions: turtles.

SNAKES (BOAS) FOR FOREST HABITAT: tree boa. Companions: same-size snakes.

SNAKES (BOAS) FOR DESERT HABITAT: sand boa. Companions: same-size snakes.

SNAKES (BOAS) FOR SHORELINE HABITAT: anaconda. Companions: same-size snakes.

TOADS: Best habitat: forest. Companions: small lizards.

TURTLES FOR DESERT HABITAT: gopher tortoise. Companions: lizards.

The rough sand boa, *Eryx conicus*. Photo by G. Marcuse.

TURTLES FOR FOREST HABITAT: wood, box. Companions: snakes.
TURTLES FOR BOG HABITAT: spotted, wood, box. Companions: frogs.
TURTLES FOR SHORELINE HABITAT: red-ear, painted. Companions: snakes.

One good way to get into this subject of terrariums is, first, to classify the various concentrated little bits of nature you want to bring into your home. Then each will be discussed separately. The classifications you were reading a moment ago are just fine for the purpose. Desert, woodland or forest, bog, shoreline or aquatic. Each is successively wetter.

DESERT is dry, with water in a container, and a screen cover.

WOODLAND is moistened earth, with a container of water and a screen cover.

BOG is peat moss, sphagnum moss or just plain ordinary everyday moss; a glass cover is provided to keep the humidity of the environment as high as in a summertime swamp.

False hognose snake, *Lioheterodon modestus,* Madagascar. Photo by H. Hansen, Aquarium Berlin.

Banded krait, *Bungarus fasciatus*. Photo by G. Marcuse.

Tentacled snake, *Herpeton tentacularum*. Photo by J. K. Langhammer.

SHORELINE is best achieved in an aquarium. Water and land are about equally divided, and a ramp or gentle slope connects the two. So much water is present that humidity is usually no problem, and any cover will do.

The fifth category, AQUATIC, is 100% water but really, this gets to be an aquarium. It is, however, used for some mud, musk and softshell aquatic turtles, aquatic salamanders such as the mud-puppy and the sirens, and even a few snakes!

Although most of the herptiles mentioned here are native to North America, the arrangement of terrariums anywhere in the world is the same, once you decide on the habitat you wish to imitate.

THE BASIC BOX

When you look to buy, you should start by deciding the habitat and size required. These factors have already been mentioned. Now comes the problem of choosing the material the terrarium is made from. There is not too much choice if you decide to buy a ready-made terrarium. If you want to *look* in, at least one opening must be glass or clear plastic or screen. If the habitat is wetter than a woodland, the bottom two or three inches must be absolutely watertight because what doesn't leak out will surely sweat out.

Some of the terrariums on the market are made with clear plastic windows, and these work just fine too. They are less likely to break, but they are more readily scratched. So you pay your money and you take your choice.

The best shoreline or aquatic terrarium is a fish aquarium. If you plan on turtles or shoreline habitat, choose a low tank; the square inches of floorspace are more useful to your squat pets than a big capacity in a tall shape. Of course if your shoreline or bog is to have tree frogs, the tall tank would be quite appropriate.

Regardless of shape, you should look for a well-made product with no sharp edges inside or outside. Try to get one with a metal or plastic frame over the top edges of the glass. This will reduce the possibility of broken glass when you lift the cover and then accidentally let it slip through your fingers. It happens to the best of us.

An all-glass tank with a close-fitting hood makes the perfect starting unit for the simple terrarium. Photo courtesy of O'Dell Manufacturing Co., Inc.

The glass should be cleaned with any household cleaner, inside and out, when you bring your new terrarium home. After you have arranged the plants and rocks it will be rather hard to do much cleaning inside. Whatever soap or detergent or chemical you use to clean the tank, be sure to rinse it out well before you put animals in the tank.

If you decide to build your own terrarium, start with a plan designed for the habitat. Wet habitats require absolutely watertight bottom sections. You might work up from an aquarium and build a screen enclosure over it. For any enclosure that has to be watertight, you're probably well advised to purchase a regular aquarium at a petshop rather than try to get along on a makeshift item.

Shield snake, *Aspidelaps scutatus*, South Africa. Photo by H. Hansen, Aquarium Berlin.

Egyptian cobra, *Naja hajae,* northern Africa. Photo by G. Marcuse.

Arizona coral snake, *Micruroides euryxanthus,* southwestern U.S. Photo by J. K. Langhammer.

For woodland or desert settings your terrarium need not be watertight, but it should be tight enough to keep dry sand from drifting out the cracks. The base and lower sides could be sheet plastic cemented at the joints, or galvanized iron such as a tinsmith uses, or sheet aluminum which is sold in the larger hardware stores. The metal joints must be smoothly welded, brazed, soldered or riveted. Unless you are especially competent in one of these trades, you had better stick to herpetology and buy a readymade tank. Wooden bases are often attractive. Some can be lined with thin gauge roofing copper. If you plan to build a wood base terrarium, choose California redwood, cypress, teak, mahogany or some other wood known to resist dampness. Painting the inside of a wooden base terrarium with black asphaltum paint never seems to work as well as people plan it, and some of the easy-to-work-with wood preservatives contain poisons.

Screening should be carefully chosen. Snakes sometimes rub their noses raw on front screens if they get restless. For them, a glass wall terrarium with a screen cover is best. Some lizards run over a fine insect screen and make an annoying noise—especially early on a Sunday morning. For them, choose a fiberglass or plastic screen or a coarser galvanized mesh.

Covers should be planned with escapes in mind. You should think about this carefully at least once. Most herptiles think about it all the time. A two-part cover is handy when you have active climbers or jumpers. With only half the cover off when you feed or water them, the chance of your pet's escape is reduced.

ACCESSORIES

Choosing accessories is simple. First you build or buy an aquarium or terrarium. Then you close your terrarium to prevent unwanted visitors; mice, for instance, will steal pet foods such as mealworms. Cats will steal frogs. Small boys will run off with anything they can lay their grubby little hands on.

If you have a dry home and a bog habitat, you will want a glass cover to keep moisture in, enemies out. You must beware of insect sprays; many of them are deadly to terrarium pets, and even the glass cover is not 100% protection against these poisons!

Choose a cover to prevent escapes. If you keep snakes, you will discover that they are the world's greatest escape artists. They crawl to places you never dreamed they could, and then they push with strengths you never dreamed they had.

The ultimate in snake cages is of course one with controlled temperature and humidity.

Screening is fine if it is fine enough and securely fastened to a heavy frame. Aluminum screening is the safest. Galvanized steel will rust in time. Brass or bronze or copper screen tends to turn green in humid situations. Plastic with perforations is a good bet if the openings are small enough.

Lights mounted in covers are desirable. It cannot be too strongly stressed, however, that the best and safest and often cheapest lights are the kind you buy from your pet dealer. Your pet dealer will also be able to furnish you with various sizes of ready-made terrariums and aquariums, also washed gravel, nets, thermometers, and even some plants. Look at his offering *before* you start to build.

Dark sea snake, *Astrotia stokesii*, Pacific Ocean. Photo by R. Steene.

Rhinoceros viper, *Bitis nasicornis*. Photo by J. K. Langhammer.

Radde's viper, *Vipera xanthina,* Armenia. Photo by Dr. Otto Klee.

Gaboon viper, *Bitis gabonica.* Photo by J. K. Langhammer.

DESERT TERRARIUM

The desert is a habitat of contrast. It has hot, dry, brilliant light in daytime but is cool at night. With the cooling, what little moisture is in the air condenses on rocks and cactus plants for the animals to lap up before the morning sun dries it out. Rain falls, but not often. When it does rain, the plants and animals absorb what they need, as the ground quickly dries. The desert sand retains little or no dampness. Certainly the top two inches is absolutely bone dry.

This is a habitat where the reptiles dominate. Meals are infrequent. Most mammals and birds need daily food, but herptiles can thrive on one good meal a week. Some actually do better that way. Amphibians are rare in the desert because they need a land-water or 100% water environment for breeding, and this obviously is not provided by the desert. Also, their soft (in some cases slimy) bodies would quickly dry out, and death would result.

Here is the habitat of the sand boa and the horned lizard— several species are available to pet keepers. A baker's dozen of other lizards, snakes, and tortoises also thrive in desert atmospheres. Among the desert tortoises, there are the gopher and the three-toed. A Greek tortoise has been exported all over the world as a terrarium pet, and it does well in a desert or modified desert-woodland environment. North Africa also provides several interesting desert tortoises. Incidentally, all the shelled reptiles are, strictly speaking, turtles, but in the common parlance a turtle lives mostly in water, a terrapin is in-and-out, and a tortoise spends most of his time on land, but don't stake any of your money on *that*.

Getting back to the desert, here are the things you must provide to establish the habitat.

Sand to burrow in and hide under is a must. Horned lizards, also called "horned toads," revel in it. Sometimes they hide in it for days on end while they work up an appetite or wait for the sun to get warmer, or whatever. They also lay their eggs in the sand; this of course applies only to the egglaying horned lizards—some are livebearers. Some of the reptiles in your collection may be egg layers. Others, mostly among the snakes, are live bearers, but this is a subject for you to get into *after* you have established your terrarium and obtained your pets. Incidentally, don't waste any time dreaming about breeding your pets. They do it better, and cheaper, in nature. No one has grown wealthy by selling home-grown snakes. If you want to make money, try tomatoes or poultry. *Herptiles are for fun.*

Getting back to the desert sand again, you should choose something fine enough to permit easy digging but coarse enough to drain easily and not pack. Cactus will not grow in it, so plant your desert vegetation in small pots of sandy earth, and then bury the pots in the sand. Another advantage in this system is that the terrarium can be cleaned or re-arranged without disturbing the plant roots. The pots need not show. A few flat rocks are required. They hold the heat of the day to warm the animals at night. They are useful as shelters if the sunlight, or the electric light you provide, is hotter than the animals like it to be. Place the rocks so horned lizards and snakes can burrow under some; others should be tipped up to provide shelter for small tortoises or those lizards that don't burrow.

Plants are best chosen to match the habitat. Cactus comes in many styles, and the spines are no problem to the animals. Desert animals have been living with desert thorns for a long, long time. If you plan to keep iguanas or some tortoises, you may have trouble finding plants that the animals will not eat. One solution is to pot the plants and suspend the pots from the top of the terrarium. The hanging gardens of Babylon were famous—maybe yours will be too.

Soft woodland plants just cannot survive in the desert habitat. Don't waste your time trying. One garden plant which will adapt to the desert is the yucca. It apparently originated there. A small yucca or clump of seedlings might be just the thing for your desert terrarium.

The desert needs bright, hot light. If you can place your terrarium where it gets bright sunlight, do so. Then supplement the sunlight as required to keep the temperature of the top quarter-inch of sand about 90 or 95 degrees F. for at least nine hours a day.

A desert terrarium measuring 12 x 12 x 20 inches should have about 50 watts of incandescent electric lamps available for light and heat in the latitude of, say, Columbus, Ohio. In summertime, the lights may be required for one hour a day. In winter, four hours daily may be necessary. You have to be the best judge of that. Base your decision on how your pets react to

Palm viper, *Bothrops lateralis,* South America. Photo by G. Marcuse.

Russell's viper, *Vipera russelli.* Photo by H. Hansen, Aquarium Berlin.

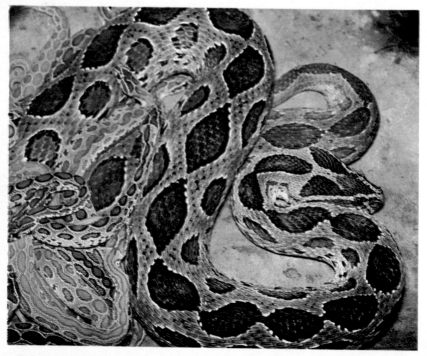

Bushmaster, *Lachesis muta*. Photo by H. Schultz.

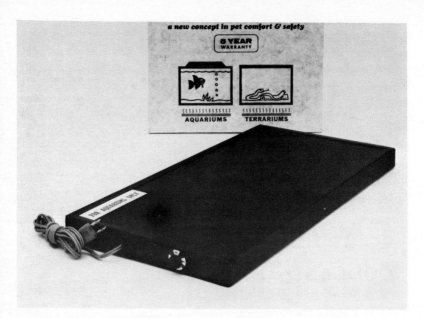

Terrarium heaters should give uniform heat across the entire bottom of the cage. Photo courtesy of Aztech International.

the warmth. Do they cluster under it, or do they try to avoid the direct rays?

The light might well be part of the cover of your terrarium. Don't try to make one without first looking at what your pet dealer has to offer. You will probably find you can get a better reflector cheaper by buying it. The top of your desert terrarium depends on your pets. Turtles and horned lizards require nothing if the sides are high and smooth. If you keep snakes, you owe it to your pets and to your family to have a *locked* cover. This sounds a little foolish to some beginning pet keepers, but when you consider the effect pet snakes have on some people, a locked cover for snake enclosures becomes imperative. Remember, your pursuit of happiness in a free nation extends only to the point where it interferes with another person's rights, and there are a few people who just aren't happy with snakes at large, even non-poisonous ones.

Water *is* necessary in the desert. The trick is to keep the sand dry, so try a deep, heavy, clean ashtray or similar dish. Some reptiles like to get wet to help them shed their old skins. The dish should be large enough to let them get wet all over and deep enough so as not to splash over when a pet crawls through it or coils up in it. Although it is not part of the terrarium, one accessory you should have is a spray of some sort for water. Some reptiles will learn to drink from a dish. Others get their water from juicy fruits and vegetables, but some don't ever get the hang of drinking from a dish. For them, a droplet of water (like dew) on a leaf or rock is just their cup of tea. Some animals, such as the horned "toads" and many desert toads, absorb their water through the skin and should be lightly sprayed with a fine mist every few days. Be very careful that any water bowls in the terrarium are not so deep that a small lizard can drown in it; remember that many desert animals never see large amounts of standing water.

WOODLAND TERRARIUM

Woodland is intermediate between desert and bog. The earth is barely moist, and the sunlight is filtered or at least weaker than that of the desert. More water is available for plant growth, and the temperature change from day to night is not so severe. This is the habitat of the wood and box turtles, the warty toads. Frogs like the pickerel and wood frogs sometimes appear in it; the garter, green, milk and hognose snakes are at home here. So are the skinks and some fence lizards. Also the American chameleon. Some terrestrial newts live under rocks in a woodland habitat. It is simple to set up and provide a home for a great variety of interesting animals.

The temperature should be like a temperate summer, 65-70° F. at night and 75-80° F. daytimes, for North American herptiles. Most boas do better at 80-82° F. daytimes and perhaps 78° F. at night. Humidity need not be controlled, since the amphibians will absorb moisture from the water dish or the soil, and the reptiles will not be baked much, since the sunlight is not nearly as hot as that of the desert climate.

Plants in woodland can be anything from philodendron to seedling cedars. The stems should be tough enough to support the climbers, resilient enough to spring back after a tortoise crawls over them. This rules out geraniums, begonias and most annuals. The snakes and toads often uproot plants. One way to stop this is to pot the plants and then weight the pots down with heavy stones.

Copperhead, *Agkistrodon contortrix*, two subspecies. Photo by G. Marcuse.

Cantil, *Agkistrodon bilineatus*. Photo by J. K. Langhammer.

Eastern pigmy rattlesnake, *Sistrurus miliaris miliaris*. Photo by J. K. Langhammer.

The soil might well be garden topsoil with a provision for a water dish large enough for your pet to crawl in and sloped properly to permit it to crawl out again. Situate it so it can be cleaned or changed frequently. It is surprising how quickly still water in a terrarium will stagnate. The smell produced will quickly cause you, or your pets, to leave home.

Large slabs of bark or slate shingle are appropriate, and snakes and lizards like to sun themselves on them and hide under them. Be sure, as you add plants and stones, to leave enough clear space in your terrarium for the largest specimen to move about comfortably.

BOG TERRARIUM

This is the home of the red eft and the spotted turtle, the ribbon snake, the wood frog, the spring peeper and the tree frogs. A large selection of "woodland" salamanders are also at home in the bog. This environment is intermediate between the woodland and the shoreline with respect to moisture. It is the region of ground pine, sphagnum moss, peat moss, ferns, skunk cabbage and jack-in-the-pulpit.

Hot direct sun never reaches the ground. Water should be contained in a dish large enough to permit animals to soak their bodies completely by crawling into it. Amphibians such as frogs, toads and salamanders don't drink through their mouths, but through their skins. They sit in rain or in a dish of clean water for a half hour or so, now and then, and this gives them the water they need. Water also helps some terrarium pets to shed their skins periodically. One precaution: don't keep leopard or pickerel frogs in with all your other frogs until you have carefully tested them. Some leopard or pickerel frogs seem to secrete a poison into the water which will kill the other species. On the other hand, you may discover that you can keep pickerel frogs with some snakes, because this secretion is so distasteful the snakes won't eat a second one in their lifetime.

The bog does not need artificial light if you keep it in a room of your home. In fact, direct sunlight for one hour a day is the maximum for a bog habitat. Again, the plants should be potted if snakes or turtles are kept.

If you house only salamanders and frogs and tiny skinks, the plants can be rooted directly in the terrarium if you prefer. Most pet keepers like to rearrange now and then; if you are that way, potted plants will make this re-decoration much easier.

For a bog terrarium with just spring peepers or other small frogs you might want to try some orchids for vegetation —or African violets. These are no good with large or heavy pets, but a small tree frog does just fine on the leaf of a hardy native orchid.

A cover is a must. Some salamanders, many frogs and most snakes climb. Frogs jump, too, and nothing is quite as discouraging as a dried frog under the radiator or behind a sofa. . . especially a *rare* dried frog. In wintertime the air in most homes is too dry for bog conditions. Then a glass cover is a must. A two-part cover is better still, because with it you can open just half when you feed or water your pets, and the chance of the prize specimen's escaping is reduced. They still do escape, but less often.

Concerning escapes, one other point is appropriate here. *An escaped snake is embarassing. An escaped venomous snake is CRIMINAL.* I feel that no pet keeper has the moral right to keep a poisonous snake in a home. Laboratory, zoo, institution of learning, yes. Home, no. Experts have been bitten. Some have lost their lives. The amateur pet keeper or his neighbor is certainly no more immune than a museum curator.

When you arrange your bog habitat you should have one area which is deep with a soft sphagnum moss, or peat moss. Three inches of moist moss is a good figure to start with. As time goes on you may find that your pets need even more moss to satisfy them. This vitally important moisture content of the moss will depend on how much it is sprinkled, the sort of terrarium cover and the temperature. Here is the point in pet keeping where the book must leave off and the interested and observant terrarium keeper takes over. Ideally, the bog is humid—yes; but wet—no. So provide a large deep dish with gentle sloping sides and keep it filled with clean fresh water. Arrange the dish so you can change the water frequently without too much trouble. Some of your bog pets may have come from muddy environments, but for an odor-free home terrarium, there is no place for stagnant mud.

Southern pigmy rattlesnake, *Sistrurus miliaris barbouri.* Photo by F. J. Dodd, Jr.

Western pigmy rattlesnake, *Sistrurus miliaris streckeri.* Photo by F. J. Dodd, Jr.

Massasauga, *Sistrurus catenatus*. Photo by J. K. Langhammer.

Eastern diamondback rattlesnake, *Crotalus adamanteus*. Photo by F. J. Dodd, Jr.

SHORELINE TERRARIUM

This is the habitat of the water snake, the green frog, the bullfrog, the eft, many salamanders and the ever-popular red ear and painted turtles. The crocodilians also abide in this sort of abode. Water and land are about equally divided. The trick is to arrange the setting so that the water can be siphoned off when uneaten food or excretions or mud begins to accumulate in the water. There are several techniques.

(A) Gravel can be sloped.

(B) Large flat rocks can be tilted to provide a ramp and dry area.

(C) A barrier of wood or glass can be arranged across the bottom, and sand can be kept on one side, water on the other.

(D) A large water container can be buried in gravel. In this, and in (C) above, a ramp must be provided.

(E) An aquarium can be furnished with potted bog plants and the water level kept at the top of the pots.

Five methods. All work. Methods A and D are popular; both hope to look natural but entail the most work in cleaning and changing water. Methods B and E are easiest to maintain. Method C is a compromise in both effect and effort. Often the glass partition in method C is arranged diagonally from corner to opposite corner in an aquarium. The edges of the partition glass should be rubbed with a wet grindstone or file to eliminate any sharp edges.

Shoreline means not only swim area, but *wet* land too. A watertight aquarium is a must for this environment. Choose the size recommended for the pet you plan to keep and while you are at it, arrange for the appropriate covering.

You say—"Three-inch turtles can't climb *up* a ten-inch glass wall." True, but a cat can crawl *down*. And so can a pet keeper's young brother. Also, the cover can often do double duty as a source of light and warmth. Many of the shoreline animals like a temperature of 75° to 85° F. in the daytime. A cover with an electric light and reflector can be chosen to light your pets, help plants grow, keep the temperature up, cover the terrarium to reduce water loss due to evaporation, and keep out domestic pets and other enemies. If snakes are kept, a wire screen should be placed over the terrarium and the light mounted *above* the screen. Anything less will lead to escapes or other disasters. You can make this light-with-reflector arrangement. This way, you will however, lose a lot of money and probably come close to electrocuting yourself and/or your pets before you finally turn to your pet dealer. He can help you select a reflector-cover which looks neater and is electrically safer than what you can build for twice the price.

AQUATIC TERRARIUM (AQUARIUM)

Strictly speaking, an aquarium is a 100% aquatic environment. No land—no terrarium. But since most people think of aquariums for fish and terrariums for herptiles, and this chapter is about beginning a herptile abode, we should consider what is necessary for an aquatic terrarium.

First of all, the best container is an all-glass or a metal-framed glass aquarium. If you plan to keep it in a cold part of your home, you should plan to provide supplementary heat in wintertime. A temperature of 75° F. is appropriate for soft-shell turtles, hellbenders, sirens, mud puppies and the few swamp snakes that are nearly aquatic. If your room is 60° F.

Many different styles of aquarium heaters are available for the aquatic terrarium or aquarium. Photo courtesy of O'Dell Manufacturing Co., Inc.

Western diamondback rattlesnake, *Crotalus atrox*. Photo by F. J. Dodd, Jr.

Mojave rattlesnake, *Crotalus scutulatus*, southwestern U.S. Photo by F. J. Dodd, Jr.

Prairie rattlesnake, *Crotalus viridis viridis.* Photo by F. J. Dodd, Jr.

Prairie rattlesnake, *Crotalus viridis nuntius.* Photo by F. J. Dodd, Jr.

or 65° F. in wintertime, you will need to provide additional warmth. An ordinary thermostatically controlled aquarium heater is ideal for this purpose. The thermostat controls the heater. You should check the heat with a thermometer daily.

So far, you have a watertight aquarium, a heater if necessary, a thermometer to check it, and what else? Simple: a cover to keep pets in, enemies out.

Also, you should provide a float or landing of some sort for those aquatic pets that sometimes change their minds. A half waterlogged stick or a large piece of cork bark, such as florists sometimes use with vines, works just fine.

The bottom should be bare or thinly covered with aquarium gravel. Mud is to be avoided; it will cloud the water, and your pets will be ever invisible.

A word of caution. No aquarium larger than one gallon should be moved when it is full. First clean it. Then place it on the flat and level stand where it is to remain. Then fill it from a pail or a hose. A perfectly good, well-made aquarium can be ruined if it is moved full or filled on an irregular surface.

SNAKES IN "OUR WORLD"

The earth was once dominated by reptiles. Snakes never led the other reptiles—they are a rather recent development. Today reptiles are in the minority. Although the tides of life ebb and flow, each creature contributes his share to the overall scheme. To wipe out or even decimate any segment of life will invariably create an imbalance which will cause trouble elsewhere. Snakes are a case in point. Almost everywhere the enemies of the mouse, rat, mole, shrew and vole have been practically exterminated. There is a bounty on foxes, mink are trapped, weasels are despised as chicken killers, and hawks are shot out of the sky. The rodents' enemies are on the run, and man is losing millions of tons of grain and other foodstuffs to the destructive powers of mice and rats.

One of the remaining controls over these rodents is the harmless snake population. For every snake a farmer kills, he must set, and keep set, several more traps. Snakes are cheaper, and they require no resetting, no oiling, no cheese. A man who kills every snake on sight shows woeful ignorance and writes a bill all of us must pay.

FOR MORE ABOUT SNAKES

For more thorough treatment of the subject, the author suggests the following general but basic books. All are easily readable and not too technical, and most can be found in high school or college libraries or purchased in used book stores.

Ditmars, Raymond L.—There are about a dozen books by him, varying from straightforward accounts of taxonomy and natural history such as *Snakes of the World* and *Reptiles of the World* to books of amusing and fascinating experiences with snakes and other animals, such as *Strange Animals I Have Known*. All these volumes are quite old (before 1930, generally) so the scientific names are often outdated.

Oliver, James A.—His book entitled *Amphibians and Reptiles of North America* contains a resume of many interesting observations and a wealth of scientific work on the subject and includes valuable snake lore and background experience from the New York Zoological Society, where Dr. Oliver was Curator of Reptiles at the Bronx Park Zoo.

Pope, Clifford H.—Mr. Pope was one of the few authorities on the reptiles of China, was long with the Philadelphia Zoo, and was an expert on salamanders, but he will probably be best remembered for his delightful books for budding herpetologists. The classic work *Snakes Alive, and How They Live* should be in every snake-keeper's library.

As mentioned earlier, there are several small guides to snake and other herptile identification available in any library or book store, as well as more elaborate state and regional manuals. At least one of these should be available to the interested collector.

In addition, T.F.H. Publications published certain books that would have an even greater degree of applicability to the interests of keepers of pet snakes, because they are books primarily involved with the keeping and maintenance of snakes and other herptiles and less with their morphology and taxonomy. Two such books are: *Snakes as Pets,* by Dr. Hobart M. Smith, $5.95, T.F.H. Publications style #AP-925 and *The Encyclopedia of Reptiles and Amphibians*, by John F. Breen, $20.00, T.F.H. Publications style # H-935.

Sidewinder, *Crotalus cerastes,* southwestern deserts. Photo by F. J. Dodd, Jr.

Rock rattlesnake, *Crotalus lepidus,* southwestern Texas to Arizona and Mexico. Photo by J. K. Langhammer.